The Drug Awareness Library™

Danger:
DRUGS AND YOUR PARENTS

E. Rafaela Picard

The Rosen Publishing Group's
PowerKids Press™
New York

Published in 1997 by The Rosen Publishing Group, Inc.
29 East 21st Street, New York, NY 10010

First Edition

Book Design: Erin McKenna

Photo Illustrations: Cover and photo illustrations by Seth Dinnerman.

Picard, E. Rafaela.
    Danger: Drugs and your parents / E. Rafaela Picard.
       p.   cm. — (The drug awareness library)
    Includes index.
    Summary: Discusses how the disease of chemical dependency in a parent can affect families and how children can get help.
    ISBN 0-8239-5050-6
    1. Parents—Substance use—Juvenile literature. 2. Substance abuse—Juvenile literature. [1. Substance abuse. 2. Family problems.] I. Title. II. Title: Drugs and your parents. III. Series.
HV4999.P37P53 1997
362.29'13—dc21
                                      96-40329
                                          CIP
                                          AC

Manufactured in the United States of America

Contents

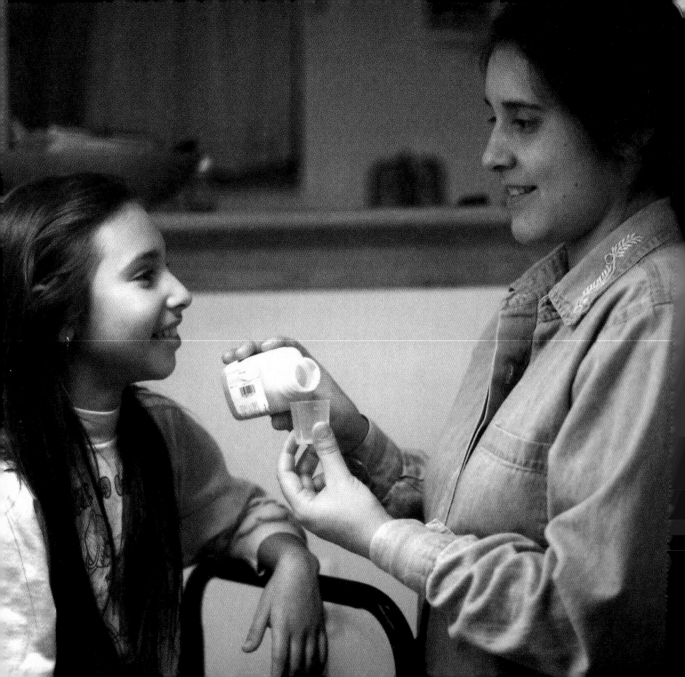

What Is a Drug?

A drug is something that changes the way a person thinks, feels, or acts. Some drugs can hurt people who use them. These drugs include alcohol as well as drugs that are sold **illegally** (il-LEE-gul-lee), such as cocaine, heroin, and crack. Other drugs can help your body. They are called medicines. When you are sick, your parent or your doctor may give you medicine to help you get well.

People sometimes **abuse** (uh-BYOOZ) medicines, other drugs, or alcohol.

◀ Medicines can help you get well when you are sick.

Chemical Dependence

Some people who abuse drugs or alcohol have a disease called **chemical dependence** (KEM-ih-kul dee-PEN-dents). A person who has chemical dependence feels the need to use alcohol or drugs again and again. She may not be drunk or "**high**" (HY) all the time. But when she uses drugs or alcohol, she loses control over how much she uses. Chemical dependence on drugs is known as **drug addiction** (DRUG uh-DIK-shun). Chemical dependence on alcohol is called **alcoholism** (AL-kuh-hol-izm).

A person who has chemical dependence can't control her use of drugs or alcohol. ▶

Changes in Behavior

Chemical dependence changes people's **behavior** (be-HAYV-yor). A parent who has chemical dependence may not wake up even though the alarm clock keeps ringing. He may not shop for groceries or cook dinner. He may sound strange when he talks. He may yell at his children for things they didn't do. He may go out for hours or days at a time without saying where he is going. He may not notice if his children do their homework or if they have clean clothes to wear or food to eat.

◀ The child of a parent with chemical dependence may have to do many things, such as laundry, for himself.

Confusing Behavior

A parent with chemical dependence may be happy one minute and angry the next. Her mood may suddenly change. The child of this person may never know what to expect.

A parent with the disease may promise that she will not use the drug anymore. But she may use it again anyway. She may promise to go to a Little League game, but she may forget to show up. It is hard to trust a parent who has chemical dependence.

It can feel bad when a parent forgets something she was supposed to do with you. ▶

Abuse

Some parents with chemical dependence abuse their children. A parent may tell his child that he doesn't care about her. He may hit her. He may lock her in her room, or not feed her enough. He may leave her alone in the house for several hours or even days.

But no child *ever* deserves to be abused. It is important for you to be safe. That's why it is good to learn all you can about chemical dependence. You can take care of yourself by talking to someone about the abuse.

◀ It can be scary and painful if your parent abuses you.

13

It's Not Your Fault

Chemical dependence is a disease. If your parent has this disease, it is important to remember that:

- You did not cause your parent to have it.
- You cannot control it.
- You cannot cure it.

You cannot change your parent's behavior. But you can do something that's very important. You can help yourself and your family by finding help.

14

Denial

A parent with chemical dependence may do things that hurt her family. Then she may pretend that she's not doing them. This is called **denial** (dee-NY-ul). When a person has chemical dependence, denial becomes a big part of her life. Denial usually **affects** (uh-FEKTS) the whole family. Other family members may also pretend that everything is okay. They may make **excuses** (ek-SKYOO-sez) for the person with chemical dependence.

◀ Many families try hard to pretend that everything is okay, even when it isn't.

Talk About It

If your parent has chemical dependence, you may have learned to pretend that everything is okay. You may have been told that it is bad to tell anyone what is going on in your home. And you may have learned that it is not safe to talk about how you feel. But if you keep your feelings locked inside, you will feel more confused. Talking about your feelings and what's going on at home will help you feel better.

Talking to an adult you trust can help make you feel better. ▶

Finding Help

If you think your parent has chemical dependence, talk to an adult you trust. Many people want to help you and your family. Talk to a friend's parent, your favorite teacher, a minister or rabbi, or a school counselor. Your safety is important. If your parent is drunk or high and loses control and hurts you, it is important to tell someone. You can tell a neighbor, or call 911 or the police. These people may also be able to help your parent.

◀ You're not alone. There are lots of other kids who feel the same way you do.

You Are Not Alone

You may think that your family is the only one that acts this way. But many families have this problem. Many kids feel the way you do. And many families have gotten help. Your parent is the only one who can solve his or her problem of chemical dependence. He or she needs help. But he or she must want help to get better. You cannot change your parent's behavior. But you can take care of yourself by talking to an adult you trust.

Glossary

abuse (uh-BYOOZ) To treat somebody or use something in a way that is harmful.

affect (uh-FEKT) To have an impact on someone or something.

alcoholism (AL-kuh-hol-izm) The disease in which someone has a chemical dependence on alcohol.

behavior (be-HAYV-yor) How someone acts.

chemical dependence (KEM-ih-kul dee-PEN-dents) The disease of not being able to control the use of drugs or alcohol.

denial (dee-NY-ul) Pretending that something is not happening when it really is.

drug addiction (DRUG uh-DIK-shun) The disease where someone has a chemical dependence on a drug.

excuse (ek-SKYOOS) Reason used to explain why something has happened.

high (HY) A false feeling of happiness when using a drug.

illegally (il-LEE-gul-lee) To do something that is against the law.

23

Index